Animals

Los animales

lohs ah-nee-*mah*-lehs

Illustrated by Clare Beaton

Ilustraciones de Clare Beaton

BARRON'S

cat

el gato, la gata

ehl *gah*-toh, lah *gah*-tah

(In Spanish, most male animals' names end in **o**, and most female animals' names end in **a**.)

dog

el perro, la perra

ehl *pehr*-roh, lah *pehr*-rah

horse

el caballo

ehl kah-*bah*-yoh

COW

la vaca

lah *vah*-kah

rabbit

el conejo, la coneja

ehl koh-*neh*-hoh, lah koh-*neh*-hah

sheep

la oveja

lah oh-*veh*-hah

goat

la cabra

lah *kah*-brah

chicken

la gallina

lah gah-*yee*-nah

mouse

el ratón, la ratona

ehl rat-*tohn*, lah rah-*toh*-nah

pig

el cerdo, la cerda

ehl *sehr*-doh, lah *sehr*-dah

duck

el pato, la pata

ehl *pah*-toh, lah *pah*-tah

A simple guide to pronouncing Spanish words

- Read this guide as naturally as possible, as if it were English.
- Put stress on the letters in *italics*, for example, *neh* in koh-*neh*-hoh.

Los animales	lohs ah-nee-*mah*-lehs	**Animals**
el gato, la gata	ehl *gah*-to, lah *gah*-tah	**cat**
el perro, la perra	ehl *pehr*-roh, lah *pehr*-rah	**dog**
el caballo	ehl kah-*bah*-yoh	**horse**
la vaca	lah *vah*-kah	**cow**
el conejo,	ehl koh-*neh*-hoh,	**rabbit**
la coneja	lah koh-*neh*-hah	
la oveja	lah oh-*veh*-hah	**sheep**
la cabra	lah *kah*-brah	**goat**
la gallina	lah gah-*yee*-nah	**chicken**
el ratón,	ehl rah-*tohn*,	**mouse**
la ratona	lah rah-*toh*-nah	
el cerdo, la cerda	ehl *sehr*-doh, lah *sehr*-dah	**pig**
el pato, la pata	ehl *pah*-toh, lah *pah*-tah	**duck**